ANTARCTICA
THE FROZEN CONTINENT

GREG REID

Smart Apple Media

To Kathy, Steve, Sam and Mia.

This edition first published in 2005 in the United States of America by Smart Apple Media.

Smart Apple Media
1980 Lookout Drive
North Mankato
Minnesota 56003

First published in 2005 by
MACMILLAN EDUCATION AUSTRALIA PTY LTD
627 Chapel Street, South Yarra, Australia 3141

Visit our website at www.macmillan.com.au

Associated companies and representatives throughout the world.

Library of Congress Cataloging-in-Publication Data
Reid, Greg, 1955-
    The Frozen Continent / by Greg Reid
    p. cm, -- (Antarctica)
    Includes index
    ISBN 1-58340-761-8   3952 3989 02/09
    1. Antarctica--Juvenile literature. 1. Title.
    G863.R392 2005
    919.8'9--dc22

                                                    2005042583

Edited by Vanessa Lanaway
Text and cover design by Ivan Finnegan, iF Design
Illustrations on pages 5 and 14 by Ivan Finnegan, iF Design
Illustrations on pages 20 and 26 by Richard Morden
Maps by Laurie Whiddon, Map Illustrations
Photo research by Jes Senbergs

Printed in China

Acknowledgments

The author would like to thank the following people for their invaluable help: Angela Berry,
Beryl Hansen, Louise Harris, Carmen Galvin, Janine Hanna, Sandra McMullan, Eileen Shuttleworth,
Joanna Taylor, Cathryn Williams, Eunice Wong.

The author and the publisher are grateful to the following for permission to reproduce copyright
material:

Front cover photographs: Satellite image of the continent of Antarctica, showing areas of thick
ice and land but not the permanent ice shelves surrounding the continent, courtesy of Worldsat
International/Science Photo Library.

Pancake ice (left), courtesy of D. Parer & E. Parer-Cook/Auscape. Blue berg (middle), courtesy
of Global Publishing. Antarctic Peninsula (right), courtesy of Tui De Roy/Auscape.

Back cover photograph: Transantarctic Mountains, courtesy of Jean Paul Ferrero/Auscape.

Tui De Roy/Auscape, p. 19; Jean Paul Ferrero/Auscape, p. 18; D. Parer & E. Parer-Cook/Auscape,
pp. 11, 22; Rick Price–Survival Anglia/Auscape, p. 23; William Sutton/Auscape, p. 15; Corbis,
p. 25; Global Publishing, pp. 16, 24; Hedgehog House, p. 17; Dr Nick Gales/Lochman
Transparencies, p. 28; Reg Morgan, pp. 13, 30; NASA, p. 29; Patricia Selkirk, pp. 4, 27;
British Antarctic Survey/Science Photo Library, pp. 12 (right), 21.

Background and header images courtesy of www.istockphoto.com. Frozen Fact background image
courtesy of NOAA.

Please note

Contents

GLOSSARY WORDS
When a word is printed in bold, you can look up its meaning in the Glossary on page 31.

Look for this symbol to find links to more information online.

The Antarctic

The Antarctic consists of the frozen continent of Antarctica, the stormy Southern Ocean, and the isolated **sub-Antarctic islands**. The region is the world's last great wilderness and contains unique landscapes, plants, and animals.

Antarctica is one of the harshest environments for life on Earth. It is an island continent that is mostly buried under snow and ice. Antarctica has a thick **ice sheet** and thousands of **valley glaciers**, floating **ice shelves**, ice cliffs, sea ice, and icebergs. Its isolation and cold climate protected it from discovery for many years.

No country owns Antarctica, but several countries have claimed parts of Antarctica and the sub-Antarctic islands. There are scientific research stations on Antarctica and some of its surrounding islands. Tourists also visit Antarctica to see its beauty and wildlife. Today, the continent has become a unique place of international cooperation. Managing the Antarctic is a major issue for all countries, both now and in the future.

The continent of Antarctica is a frozen wilderness.

FROZEN FACT

ANCIENT PREDICTION

The ancient Greeks believed there was a great southern continent. They called the constellation of stars above the northern sky *Arctos* or "the bear," so they called the southern continent *Antarktikos* or "opposite the bear."

WHAT MAKES ANTARCTICA UNIQUE?

There are many things that make Antarctica unique. It is the fifth largest continent in the world, yet it was the last to be discovered and explored. Antarctica is larger than Europe and almost twice as big as Australia.

Antarctica is the coldest, driest, and windiest of all the continents. It has the world's greatest amount of ice, and is the largest cold desert. Most of Antarctica is covered by a cap of ice, called an ice sheet. The Antarctic ice sheet is the largest **continental glacier** in the world.

http://www.pbs.org/wnet/nature/antarctica/index.html

http://www.pbs.org/wgbh/nova/warnings/almanac.html

Antarctica has the greatest average height of any continent. It also has the world's longest valley glacier, Lambert Glacier, and Ross Ice Shelf, which is the largest ice shelf in the world.

Area (square miles/kilometers)

ASIA 17,225,000 square miles (44,614,000 sq km)

AFRICA 11,706,000 square miles (30,319,000 sq km)

NORTH AMERICA 9,362,000 square miles (24,247,000 sq km)

SOUTH AMERICA 6,886,000 square miles (17,834,000 sq km)

ANTARCTICA 5,500,000 square miles (13,209,000 sq km)

EUROPE 4,093,000 square miles (10,600,000 sq km)

AUSTRALIA 2,968,000 square miles (7,687,000 sq km)

Continents

The size of the continents

FROZEN FACT

LAST WILDERNESS

Antarctica and its surrounding ocean is mostly a **pristine** wilderness. Yet, despite its isolation and harsh climate, humans have had an impact on its unique landscapes, plants, and animals.

Where is Antarctica?

Antarctica is the southernmost continent in the world and surrounds the South Pole. Antarctica and Australia are the only continents that lie entirely in the southern hemisphere.

The nearest continents to Antarctica are South America, Africa, and Australia. The closest countries to Antarctica are Argentina, Chile, South Africa, New Zealand, and Australia.

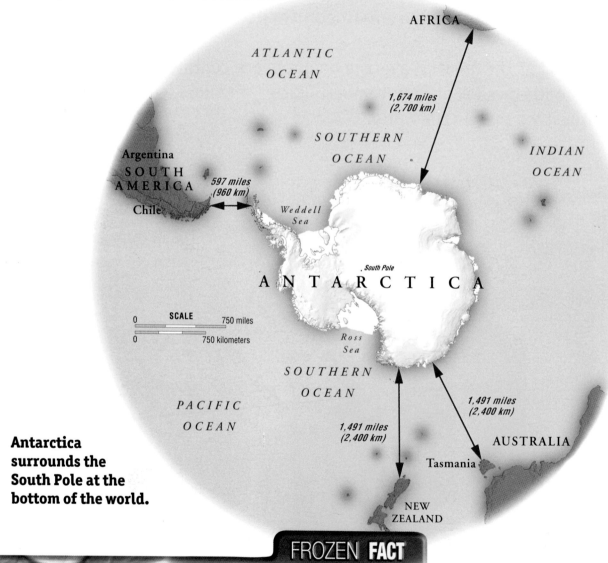

AFRICA

ATLANTIC
OCEAN

1,674 miles
(2,700 km)

SOUTHERN
OCEAN

INDIAN
OCEAN

Argentina
SOUTH
AMERICA

597 miles
(960 km)

Chile

Weddell
Sea

South Pole

ANTARCTICA

SCALE
0   750 miles
0   750 kilometers

Ross
Sea

SOUTHERN
OCEAN

PACIFIC
OCEAN

1,491 miles
(2,400 km)

1,491 miles
(2,400 km)

AUSTRALIA

Tasmania

**Antarctica
surrounds the
South Pole at the
bottom of the world.**

NEW
ZEALAND

FROZEN **FACT**

GEOGRAPHY OF ANTARCTICA
* **Antarctica lies almost entirely within the Antarctic Circle.**
* **Antarctica is about 2,790 miles (4,500 km) wide.**
* **The coastline is about 19,840 miles (32,000 km) all the way around.**

REMOTE CONTINENT

Antarctica is the most remote continent in the world. The Southern Ocean that surrounds Antarctica is the only ocean to surround a continent.

About 130 million years ago, Antarctica was joined to South America, India, Australia, and Africa. This vast southern continent was called Gondwana. Australia separated from Antarctica about 60 million years ago.

Antarctica used to be part of Gondwana, before the nearby land masses separated.

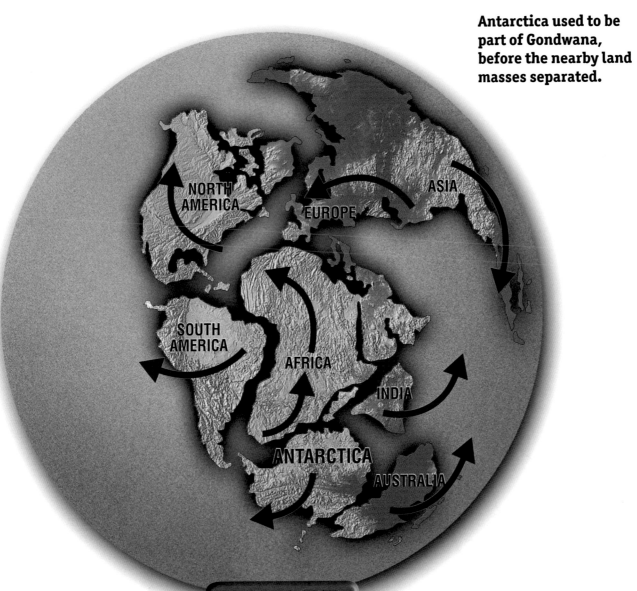

NORTH AMERICA

EUROPE

ASIA

SOUTH AMERICA

AFRICA

INDIA

ANTARCTICA

AUSTRALIA

FROZEN FACT

EXTREMOPHILES

Extremophiles are microscopic life forms, such as bacteria, algae, and yeast, that are adapted to extreme conditions. Commercial companies are taking chemicals from Antarctic extremophiles to make medical drugs, cosmetics, and food products.

Regions of Antarctica

Antarctica has many regions, including the Southern Ocean, its seas, the sub-Antarctic islands, and parts of the continent.

Major regions of Antarctica

ANTARCTIC PENINSULA

The Antarctic Peninsula was once part of the Andes Mountain range in South America. There are many extinct volcanoes in the area. The peninsula is the closest area to South America.

SOUTHERN OCEAN

The Southern Ocean is the fourth largest ocean in the world, and is the world's wildest, windiest, and coldest ocean. It completely surrounds Antarctica. Seven smaller seas, including Ross Sea and Weddell Sea form parts of the Southern Ocean.

WEDDELL SEA

The Weddell Sea is at the continent end of the Antarctic Peninsula. The Ronne, Larsen, and Filchner ice shelves lie beside the coast over part of this sea.

EAST ANTARCTICA

East Antarctica is also called Greater Antarctica. It occupies 70 percent of Antarctica and contains 90 percent of the continent's ice. Large areas of the bedrock that lies beneath the continent have been pushed more than 3,300 feet (1,000 m) below sea level under the weight of the ice sheet. East Antarctica also contains the South Pole, Transantarctic Mountains, and dry, ice-free areas called oases.

SUB-ANTARCTIC ISLANDS

Most of the islands that surround Antarctica are remote and uninhabited. A few islands have permanent research stations. Most of the sub-Antarctic islands have rich plant life and wildlife because they are warmer and wetter than Antarctica.

WEST ANTARCTICA

West Antarctica is also called Lesser Antarctica. It occupies one third of the continent. Antarctica's two highest mountains are found here in the Ellsworth Mountains. They are Vinson Massif, 16,962 feet (5,140 m) and Mt Tyree, 15,586 feet (4,723 m). West Antarctica also has active volcanoes.

ROSS SEA

The Ross Sea lies between the Transantarctic Mountains and West Antarctica. The Ross Ice Shelf is attached to the coast. There are several active volcanoes on nearby Ross Island.

TRANSANTARCTIC MOUNTAINS

This is the major mountain range in Antarctica. It separates East and West Antarctica.

Southern Ocean

The stormy Southern Ocean encircles Antarctica. It has the largest waves in the world. The Southern Ocean plays a major role in the climate of Antarctica and the world. The waters around Antarctica are called the Roaring Forties, the Furious Fifties, and the Screaming Sixties because of the fierce winds.

ANTARCTIC POLAR FRONT

The colder, saltier waters of the Southern Ocean meet the warmer waters of the northern oceans in a zone called the Antarctic Polar Front, or the Antarctic Convergence. They sink below the warmer northern waters in this 25-mile- (40-km-) wide zone.

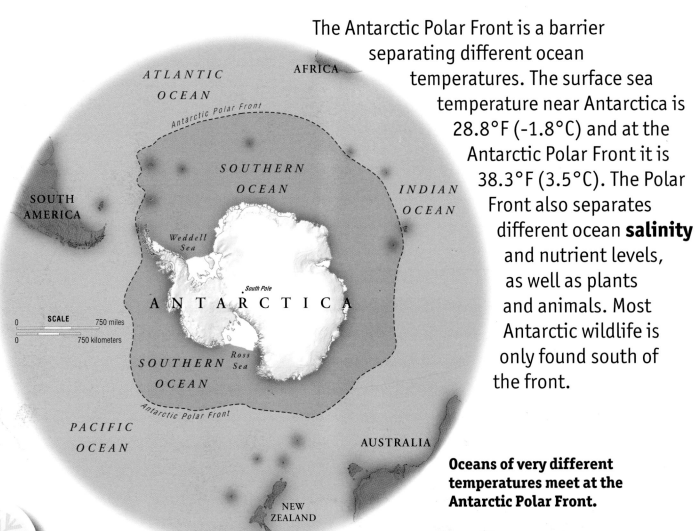

The Antarctic Polar Front is a barrier separating different ocean temperatures. The surface sea temperature near Antarctica is 28.8°F (-1.8°C) and at the Antarctic Polar Front it is 38.3°F (3.5°C). The Polar Front also separates different ocean **salinity** and nutrient levels, as well as plants and animals. Most Antarctic wildlife is only found south of the front.

Oceans of very different temperatures meet at the Antarctic Polar Front.

SEA ICE

In winter, the top layer of the ocean surrounding Antarctica freezes. This layer of sea ice is usually around three feet (1 m) thick, but can be up to 33 feet (10 m) thick.

In early winter, the surface of the sea develops ice slicks. As temperatures fall, a thin layer of sea ice forms. Wind and waves move this ice together to form circles of sea ice called pancake ice. Pancake ice eventually joins together to form pack ice, which drifts with the winds and currents offshore. Fast ice attaches itself to the edge of Antarctica, and moves up and down with the tides.

http://www.geosc.psu.edu/~dbr/Antarctica/Sea_Ice.shtml

Winter sea ice more than doubles the size of the continent. This ice barrier around Antarctica helped to make it the last continent to be discovered, because it was so difficult to get through. By summer, most of the sea ice has melted, except for sheltered areas around the coast. The area covered by sea ice varies from year to year.

Pancake ice forms on the surface of the sea at the start of winter.

FROZEN FACT

THE ELASTIC CONTINENT

In late winter, sea ice can cover an extra 7.7 million square miles (20 million sq km). In summer, sea ice only covers about 0.4 million square miles (5 million sq km).

Sub-Antarctic islands

Many groups of small islands are scattered over the vast Southern Ocean. They are rich in plant and animal life because they are warmer and wetter than Antarctica.

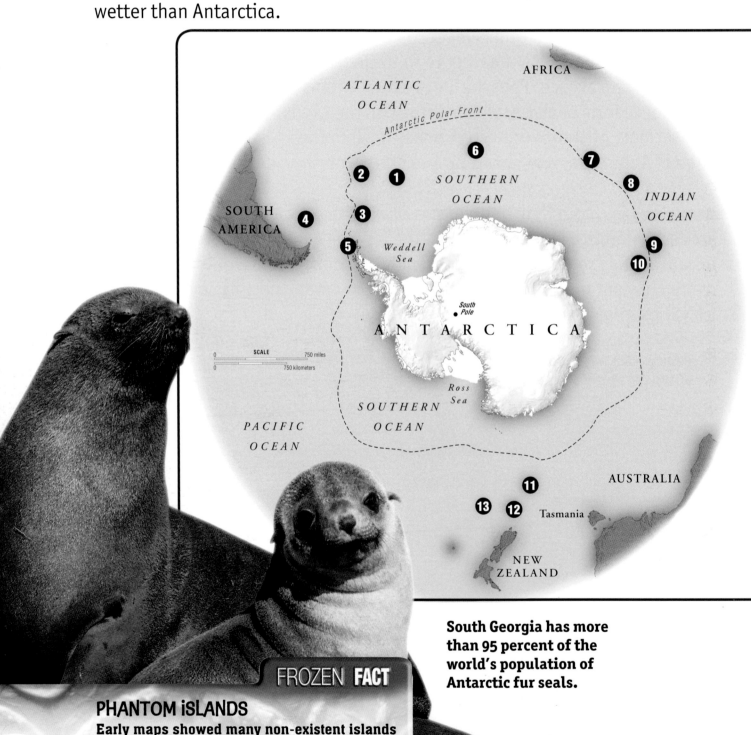

South Georgia has more than 95 percent of the world's population of Antarctic fur seals.

FROZEN **FACT**

PHANTOM ISLANDS
Early maps showed many non-existent islands in the Southern Ocean. These are called phantom islands. Today, satellites are used to prove if an island is real or not.

All of the sub-Antarctic islands are territories of the United Kingdom, France, Norway, South Africa, Australia, and New Zealand. Some islands have research bases where scientists study the climate, unique wildlife, and landscapes.

http://library.thinkquest.org/26442/html/isles/

http://www.deh.gov.au/heritage/worldheritage/sites/antarct/index.html

Major sub-Antarctic islands

❶ South Sandwich Islands (United Kingdom)

❷ South Georgia (United Kingdom)

❸ South Orkney Islands (United Kingdom)

❹ Falkland Islands (United Kingdom)

❺ South Shetland Islands (United Kingdom)

❻ Bouvet Islands (Norway)

❼ Prince Edward Islands (South Africa)

❽ Crozet Islands (France)

❾ Kerguelen Island (France)

❿ Heard and McDonald Islands (Australia)

⓫ Macquarie Island (Australia)

⓬ Auckland Islands (New Zealand)

⓭ Campbell Island (New Zealand)

Key

🐧 Wildlife
🌋 Volcanoes
❄ Glaciers
⛰ Historic relics
🔬 Major scientific base
🐬 Marine reserves
◎ World Heritage Area

FROZEN FACT

AN INSIDE-OUT ISLAND

Macquarie Island is the only island in the world made up of rocks from the ocean's crust and from deep inside the Earth's crust. The rocks were squeezed up like toothpaste from a tube about 600,000 years ago.

Climate

Antarctica is the coldest, windiest, and driest continent on Earth.

WORLD'S COLDEST CONTINENT

Antarctica is the world's coldest continent. It is extremely cold because:

❄ the snow and ice reflect back at least 85 percent of the sun's energy

❄ the sun does not shine during winter and it is dark for 24 hours a day for a few weeks of the year

❄ the continent is very high above sea level

❄ in summer, the sun is lower in the sky in Antarctica than in other areas, so Antarctica does not receive much heat. The strength of the sun's rays in Antarctica is only about 17 percent of that at the Equator.

Temperatures vary greatly from summer to winter and from the coast to the higher places inland.

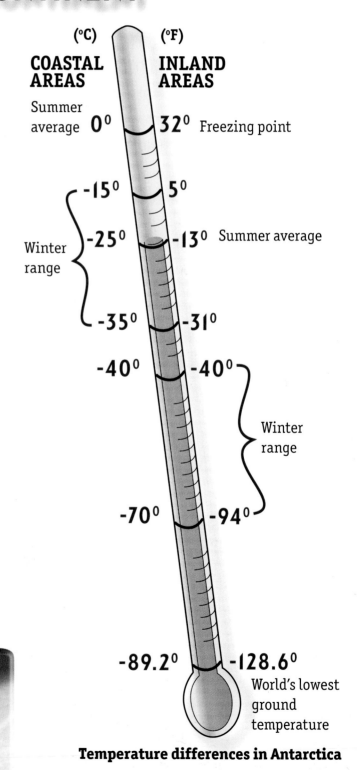

(°C)   **(°F)**

COASTAL AREAS   **INLAND AREAS**

Summer average **0°**   **32°** Freezing point

-15°   **5°**

Winter range **-25°**   **-13°** Summer average

-35°   **-31°**

-40°   **-40°**

Winter range

-70°   **-94°**

-89.2°   **-128.6°** World's lowest ground temperature

Temperature differences in Antarctica

FROZEN FACT

WORLD'S COLDEST TEMPERATURE
In 1983, scientists at Russia's Vostok base recorded the coldest ground temperature on Earth. It was -128.6°F (-89.2°C).

WORLD'S WINDIEST CONTINENT

Wind speeds can reach up to 185 miles per hour (300 kph) on the Antarctic coast. On the continent, strong winds develop when cold air drains from the high Antarctic Plateau toward the coast. These are called katabatic winds. When strong winds pick up falling or drifting snow, they form blizzards. These can sometimes last for weeks.

WORLD'S DRIEST CONTINENT

Antarctica is the world's driest and largest desert. It has around 75 percent of all the fresh water in the world, but all that water is locked away in snow and ice. Antarctica is a desert because the air is too cold to hold much water vapor. Snowfall on the Antarctic Plateau is equal to less than 2 inches (5 cm) of rainfall per year. Most snowfall is eventually compressed into ice. There is very little **evaporation** because the temperatures are so low.

http://www.aad.gov.au/default.asp?casid=1548

http://www.aad.gov.au/default.asp?casid=1546

Strong winds carve the snow into 3-feet (1-m) high, irregular ridges, called sastrugi ice.

FROZEN **FACT**
SOUTHERN LIGHTS
Southern lights, or aurora australis, are patches of colored light that occur in the sky over Antarctica. They are caused when charged particles in the solar wind react with the Earth's magnetic field.

15

Rocks

Almost all Antarctic rocks are buried under ice. These include some of the world's oldest rocks, formed 400 million years ago. More recent volcanic rocks are common in the Antarctic Peninsula.

FOSSILS

Fossils of plants and animals show that Antarctica used to be wetter and warmer when it was part of Gondwana. From these fossils, scientists know that around 150 to 40 million years ago, there were forests of southern beech, ginkgo, and conifers on Antarctica. There are even fossils of 100-million-year-old trees preserved as part of a **petrified** forest in Antarctica. The tallest "tree" is 23 feet (7m) high.

Fossil tree preserved as part of a petrified forest.

http://www.aad.gov.au/default.asp?casid=1680

http://www.abc.net.au/ozfossil/ageofreptiles/polar/default.htm

Fossils of land animals are more difficult to find. Some Antarctic dinosaurs had developed very large eyes to adapt to the long periods of winter darkness.

The ice has moved many fossils from their original areas and dumped them in other places on land and offshore. These are called recycled fossils.

FROZEN **FACT**

METEORITES
Antarctica has many unusual meteorites. Most come from asteroid fragments, but some are from Mars and the Moon. Some scientists believe that some mineral features of the meteorites from Mars show signs of life on Mars.

MINERAL RESOURCES

Antarctica is believed to have many useful mineral deposits. However, only a small percentage of the land not covered by ice has been explored for mineral deposits.

Minerals such as coal, iron ore, copper, gold, uranium, and platinum have been found in Antarctic rocks. In the Transantarctic Mountains, 13-feet- (4-m-) thick layers of coal have been found. These formed from trees and swamps that grew millions of years ago.

No detailed surveys have been conducted to see how large the mineral deposits are in Antarctica. There are also many difficulties with mining in Antarctica, because it is a remote area with a harsh climate and the rocks are mostly buried under ice.

http://www.antdiv.gov.au/default.asp?casid=6561

Coal seam in the Transantarctic Mountains

FROZEN **FACT**

MINING BAN

In 1991, to protect the **fragile** environment, an international agreement called the **Madrid Protocol** banned mining in Antarctica for 50 years. The Protocol came into force in 1998 and will be reviewed in 2048.

Mountains

The largest mountain range in Antarctica is the Transantarctic Mountains.

Antarctica is the highest continent on Earth with an average height of 7,590 feet (2,300 m) above sea level. There are several major mountain ranges, including some buried under the Antarctic ice sheet.

TRANSANTARCTIC MOUNTAINS

The Transantarctic Mountains are one of the world's great mountain chains. They are the largest mountain range in Antarctica, forming a chain of mountains, ranges and isolated **nunataks** about 1,984 miles (3,200 km) long.

The Transantarctic Mountains extend from the southwest corner of the Weddell Sea to the northwest corner of the Ross Sea. They were once part of the Andes Mountain range in South America, before the continents separated. The mountains divide the continent into East and West Antarctica. They are more than 13,200 feet (4,000 m) high and almost completely covered by snow and ice.

FROZEN FACT

HiGHEST MOUNTAiN

The highest mountain in Antarctica is Vinson Massif. It is 16,962 feet (5,140 m) high, 13 miles (21 km) long, and 8 miles (13 km) wide, and is found in the Ellsworth Mountains beside the Weddell Sea.

ANTARCTIC PENINSULA

The Antarctic Peninsula is the second major mountain range in Antarctica. It is an arc of extinct volcanoes formed at least 60 million years ago. The mountains stretch about 990 miles (1,600 km) south to Ellsworth Land where they disappear as a chain of nunataks beneath the ice sheet. The peninsula is an **archipelago** joined together and mostly covered by ice. Several ice sheets, such as Larsen and Wordie ice shelves, lie along the peninsula.

VOLCANOES

Only a few Antarctic volcanoes are active today. These include Mount Erebus on Ross Island, Mount Melbourne beside the Ross Sea, and Deception Island off the Antarctic Peninsula.

The Antarctic Peninsula is a chain of mountains that extends out from the mainland of Antarctica.

http://www.doc.ic.ac.uk/~kpt/
terraquest/va/science/geology/
geology.html#C

http://www.ees.nmt.edu/Geop/
mevo/mevo.html

http://www.ecophotoexplorers.
com/antarctica_geology.asp

FROZEN FACT

FiRE AND iCE
Snow-covered Mount Erebus is an active volcano with a molten lava lake in its crater. The volcano is 12,520 feet (3,794 m) high and is the youngest of several volcanoes forming Ross Island.

Antarctic ice sheet

The Antarctic ice sheet is a huge, dome-shaped cap of ice covering most of Antarctica. It is sometimes called the Antarctic Plateau. At an average thickness of 1.4 miles (2.2 km), the ice sheet is the world's largest continental glacier. It is formed from snow that has fallen and compressed into ice over time. Some of the ice is around 900,000 years old.

Under the ice sheet there are hidden plains, valleys, mountains, and at least 70 **sub-glacial lakes**. The ice sheet gives Antarctica the highest average height of all the continents. Without the ice sheet, Antarctica would be the lowest continent and West Antarctica would be an archipelago of three large rocky islands.

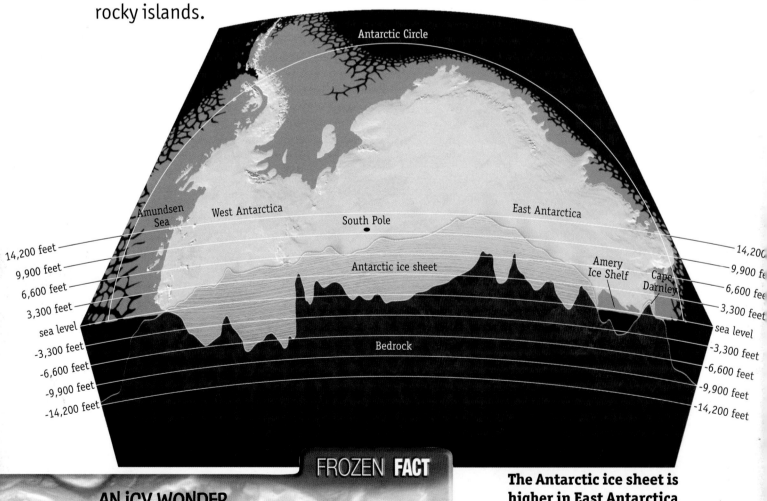

FROZEN FACT

AN iCY WONDER

The Antarctic ice sheet holds 90 percent of the world's ice and 75 percent of the world's fresh water. If the Antarctic ice sheet melted, the world's oceans would rise by about 230 feet (70 m).

The Antarctic ice sheet is higher in East Antarctica than West Antarctica.

MOVEMENT OF THE ICE SHEET

The Antarctic ice sheet flows continually outward from the center of the continent toward the ocean. It moves like a slow motion, frozen conveyor belt.

The Antarctic ice sheet creeps and slides gradually downward. As it moves, it scrapes the bedrock and carries it away. The movement of the ice sheet helps to concentrate meteorites that have fallen on the continent into certain areas. The ice sheet also removes fossils from their original locations and dumps them in other areas on land and in the sea.

http://www.secretsoftheice.org/icecore/index.html

http://www.glacier.rice.edu/land/5_antarcticicesheetintro.html

The ice sheet slides toward the ocean to form ice shelves. Eventually, icebergs break off (calve off) the edge of these ice shelves. When the icebergs melt, the water is returned to the sea. The water cycle continues when water from the sea evaporates and falls as snow on the continent.

Icebergs calve off the edge of ice shelves and melt in the sea.

FROZEN FACT

ANCIENT SECRETS

Ice traps tiny pockets of air. This air contains a record of past atmospheres and climates. Scientists drill ice cores in ancient ice and study the gases in the trapped air to see how the climate has changed.

Valley glaciers

Near mountains and valleys, the Antarctic ice sheet feeds into valley glaciers. These are slow-moving rivers of ice that flow toward the coast.

Valley glaciers are shaped like a tongue. They flow slowly and constantly downward, pulled by gravity and pushed by the weight of the ice higher up. Valley glaciers form U-shaped valleys. The glacial ice slides and creeps, grinding the bottom and sides of the valley and making it deeper and wider.

http://www.glacier.rice.edu/land/5_tableofcontents.html

FROZEN **FACT**

WORLD'S LARGEST GLACIER
Lambert Glacier carries ice from the Antarctic ice sheet to Amery Ice Shelf.
* Length: about 250 miles (400km)
* Width: more than 25 miles (40km)
* Depth: nearly 8,250 feet (2,500m).

Smaller **tributary** glaciers sometimes join larger valley glaciers. Deep cracks called crevasses form as the ice moves over steep rocky areas. Crevasses can be 100 feet (30m) across and just as deep. These are often hidden by snow and can be dangerous for people.

When a glacier reaches the sea, it either joins an ice shelf or sticks out into the sea as a glacial tongue. Eventually, pieces of the glacier will calve off to form icebergs.

ICE SHELVES

Ice shelves are flat, floating blocks of ice joined to the land on three sides. They are found in bays on almost 50 percent of the Antarctic coastline. Ice shelves are fed by glaciers, ice sheets, snow, and frozen sea ice. Some ice shelves have ice cliffs where large icebergs calve into the sea. Waves in the sea cause pressure ridges and cracks to develop in some ice shelves.

Most ice shelves are small, but there are several larger ones. The largest is Ross Ice Shelf, which extends over the Ross Sea. It is about the size of France. Ross Ice Shelf has 165-feet-high (50 m) ice cliffs facing the sea. These ice cliffs calve to form huge tabular (flat-topped) icebergs. The second largest ice shelf is Ronne Ice Shelf, which extends over the Weddell Sea.

Ice cliffs at the edge of Ross Ice Shelf.

SCALE
0 — 750 miles
0 — 750 kilometers

Riise–Larsen Ice Shelf

Weddell Sea

Filchner Ice Shelf

Larsen Ice Shelf

Wordie Ice Shelf

Ronne Ice Shelf

Amery Ice Shelf

• South Pole

ANTARCTICA

Shackleton Ice Shelf

Ross Ice Shelf

Ross Sea

Cook Ice Shelf

http://www.nsidc.org/iceshelves/
larsenb2002/index.html

FROZEN FACT

SHRINKING ICE SHELVES

The Larsen and Wordie ice shelves in the Antarctic Peninsula have greatly shrunk in recent years. Scientists think this is a result of **global warming** and the ozone hole.

Icebergs

Icebergs are lumps of freshwater ice that float in the sea. They can come from glaciers, ice shelves, and ice cliffs. There are many different types and colors of icebergs.

* Tabular icebergs are huge, flat-topped icebergs that have calved from ice shelves.

* Smaller, irregular icebergs called "growlers" break off glaciers and ice cliffs.

* Rounded icebergs are old icebergs that have rolled in the water. They often have beautiful shapes where the ocean currents have carved them.

Icebergs range in color from white to green, blue, and even pink. Blue bergs are formed from compressed glacial ice. Pink icebergs have tiny plants, called algae, in their ice. Most icebergs are white because tiny air spaces in the ice reflect white light.

http://www.glacier.rice.
edu/land/5_iceofallshapes.
html#anchor2297019

Blue bergs are rare and are formed by old glacial ice.

FROZEN FACT

GiANT iCEBERGS
In March 2000, the largest iceberg ever seen broke away from the Ross Ice Shelf. The iceberg, named B-15, was about the size of Jamaica—186 miles (300 km) long and 25 miles (40 km) wide.

MOVEMENT OF ICEBERGS

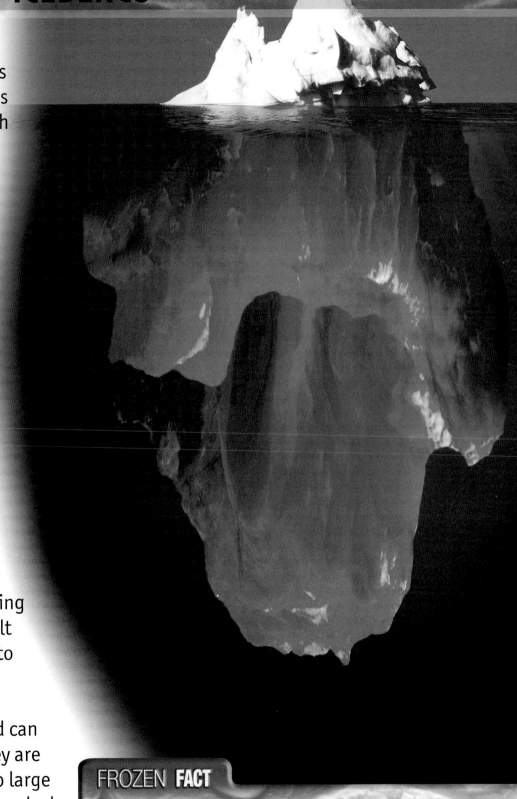

Icebergs have most of their mass under water.

There are hundreds of thousands of icebergs in Antarctic waters. Icebergs float because they are less dense than seawater. With around 80 percent of their mass under water, icebergs are moved by ocean currents rather than winds. Most drift with the current close to shore around Antarctica, but some also drift farther offshore. The average speed of an iceberg is about 7.5 miles (12 km) a day.

Icebergs in the Weddell and Ross seas move in a large, circular, clockwise direction. Many icebergs are frozen in pack ice during winter and eventually melt when they move north into warmer waters.

Icebergs are unstable and can somersault suddenly. They are hazardous to shipping, so large icebergs are continually tracked using satellite imagery.

FROZEN FACT

SEABED DAMAGE
When large icebergs calve, they scrape the seabed down to depths of about 165 feet (50 m). The slow-growing marine life is destroyed and it takes many years to grow back.

Lakes and oases

Antarctica has saltwater, freshwater, and sub-glacial lakes. Some lakes have layers of fresh and salt water. Oases in Antarctica are places that are ice-free and very dry.

LAKES IN ANTARCTICA

Saltwater lakes formed on Antarctica around 18,000 years ago. Some of these lakes are so salty that they do not freeze.

Some freshwater lakes are permanently frozen. Others are only ice-free during summer because their top layer freezes during the winter. There are at least 70 sub-glacial lakes buried under the Antarctic ice sheet.

LAKE VOSTOK

Antarctica's largest freshwater lake is Lake Vostok, hidden under the Antarctic ice sheet. It was discovered in 1996 under Russia's Vostok base. The lake is similar to oceans buried under thick layers of ice on Europa, a moon of Jupiter. It may contain ancient, unique, and unknown life forms. Scientists have stopped drilling through the ice sheet just short of the lake. They need to figure out how to protect the lake from outside influences before they continue drilling.

Lake Vostok has been buried under the Antarctic ice sheet for millions of years. In 2004, scientists found that the lake is separated into two sections.

Vostok Station
(Russian Federation)

Antarctic ice sheet

Lake Vostok

Bedrock

Lake
Vostok

OASES

Oases in Antarctica are dry, ice-free areas found mainly near the coast. They are rare, covering only two percent of the continent. The main oases are found in the Larseman, Vestfold, and Bunger hills in East Antarctica, and the Dry Valleys. Only about half an inch (1 cm) of snow falls here each year. Many oases have lakes of frozen fresh water or very saline water. Oases are extremely fragile environments that are easily damaged.

THE DRY VALLEYS

The Dry Valleys are the largest of the Antarctic oases. They are found on the western side of McMurdo Sound in the Transantarctic Mountains. No snow has fallen in this 1,170-square-mile (3,000 sq km) cold desert for at least two million years. Don Juan Pond in the Dry Valleys is so salty it never freezes. Retreating glaciers formed the Dry Valleys at the end of the last ice age around 18,000 years ago.

http://www.antarctica.ac.uk/About_Antarctica/Rock/Dry_Valleys.html

http://www.70south.com/resources/environment/vostok

http://earthsci.org/newsop/news/vostok/vostok.html

Wind has sculpted the rocks in this oasis into amazing shapes.

FROZEN FACT

MUMMiFiED SEALS
The Dry Valleys contain the remains of seals that have wandered into these oases and died. The cold, dry air preserves these seal "mummies." They may be hundreds of years old.

27

Antarctic issues

Human activities have had impacts on the unique Antarctic environment and created issues for the **ecological sustainability** of the region. Today, there is global awareness that positive action is required to protect this wilderness area.

The Antarctic Treaty is used to manage Antarctic issues. It is a unique international agreement signed by 45 nations. The Antarctic Treaty and its conventions and protocols address Antarctic issues and protect the ecological sustainability of the region.

ANTARCTIC ISSUES AND SOLUTIONS

Seal and whale hunting   The Convention for the Conservation of Antarctic Seals protects seals and manages hunting seasons. Commercial sealing no longer occurs. The International Whaling Commission has stopped all commercial whaling.

While scientists are studying wildlife, their presence has an impact on the animals.

Overfishing   The Convention for the Conservation of Antarctic Marine Living Resources controls the harvesting of marine resources. It sets catch limits and tries to control illegal fishing.

Scientific bases and research   Environmental impact agreements ensure rubbish is removed and pollution is cleaned up.

Tourism   Protocols on tourism control tourist activities and ensure that they leave nothing behind.

Introduced species   Introduced animals are no longer allowed in the Antarctic.

Mining   The Madrid Protocol banned mining for 50 years from 1998. It will be reviewed in 2048.

Global warming   The Kyoto Protocol aims to reduce greenhouse gas emissions. Several countries are investigating forms of renewable energy, such as wind power.

The ozone "hole"   The 1987 Montreal Protocol banned ozone-damaging chemicals. Ozone-friendly products are now mostly used.

GLOBAL WARMING

Burning fossil fuels such as coal, oil, and natural gas has increased the carbon dioxide levels in the atmosphere. This has caused global temperature increases. Warmer temperatures have resulted in changes to snowfall and ice cover. Melting Antarctic ice could cause global sea levels to rise by three feet (1 m) this century, which will flood low-lying areas. The Kyoto Protocol aims to control the amount of carbon emissions, but several industrial countries, such as Australia and the United States, have not signed the Protocol.

THE OZONE "HOLE"

The ozone layer protects the planet from harmful ultraviolet (UV) radiation. The ozone has been destroyed by chloro-fluoro-carbons (CFCs). CFCs are chemicals that were used in air conditioners, aerosols, and refrigerators until 1987.

The Montreal Protocol on Substances that Deplete the Ozone Layer aims to limit global CFC production. More than 155 nations have signed the protocol. Alternative ozone-friendly products are now mostly used. In 2004, a satellite was put into orbit around the Earth to monitor ozone changes. It will take many years before the "hole" in the ozone layer is repaired.

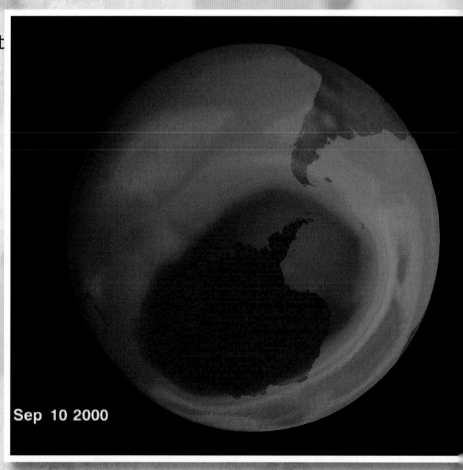

Sep 10 2000

The ozone "hole" over Antarctica

The future of the Antarctic

Antarctica holds the secrets to the Earth's past and could help us predict its future. Antarctic issues need to be fully understood and carefully managed. Many people would like to see Antarctica as a **World Heritage Area** where it would continue to be a model of peace and cooperation for the whole world.

ANTARCTIC COOPERATION

Antarctica is a unique place where scientists from all over the world live and work together in a spirit of cooperation in the wilderness. During the International Geophysical Year, from July 1957 until December 1958, scientists cooperated on many research projects. The success of this led to a permanent agreement on Antarctica, the Antarctic Treaty. Scientists are exploring how the continent has changed over time and how it continues to change today and into the future. The results of their shared work may influence the future of the planet.

http://www.antarctica.ac.uk/About_Antarctica/Conservation/

http://www.biosbcc.net/ocean/AAimportance.htm

Scientists from around the world work together in Antarctica.

Glossary

archipelago	a chain of islands
continental glacier	a slow-moving river of ice that flows over a large area
ecological sustainability	the ability of the ecosystems to stay in balance now and into the future
evaporation	when moisture (water, snow, ice) changes to water vapor
fragile	easily damaged
global warming	a global increase in air temperature caused by carbon dioxide released into the atmosphere when we burn fossil fuels such as coal and oil
ice sheet	the thick layer of ice covering most of Antarctica; also called the Antarctic Plateau
ice shelves	layers of floating ice that are still attached to the mainland on three sides
nunataks	an Inuit name for a mountain peak or a hill surrounded by ice
petrified	turned to stone
pristine	unspoilt and natural
Madrid Protocol	an agreement between nations to protect Antarctica from mining
salinity	the saltiness of water
sub-Antarctic islands	islands surrounding Antarctica
sub-glacial lakes	lakes that lie buried under the Antarctic ice sheet
tributary	a stream, river, or glacier that flows into a larger stream, river, or glacier
valley glaciers	slow-moving rivers of ice
World Heritage Area	special areas with outstanding natural and cultural values that are important to the world and have to be protected for the future

Index